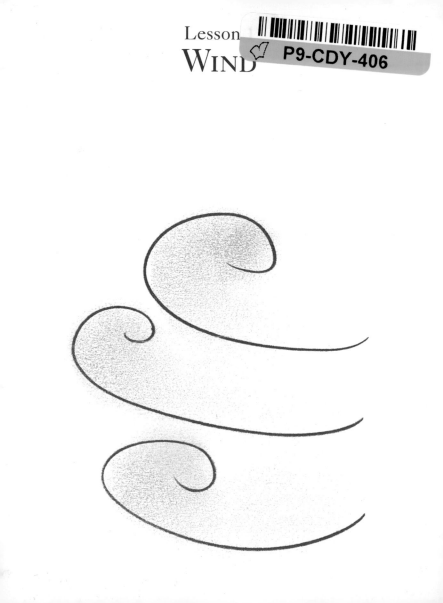

Published by Crown Publishers, a division of Random House, Inc.,
1540 Broadway, New York, N.Y. 10036

CROWN and colophon are trademarks of Random House, Inc.
www.randomhouse.com/kids
Library of Congress Catalog Card Number 00-031414

ISBN 0-517-80097-7
August 2000
Printed in Hong Kong
10 9 8 7 6 5 4 3 2 1   *First Edition*

Squeaky Chalk

Joy Sikorski

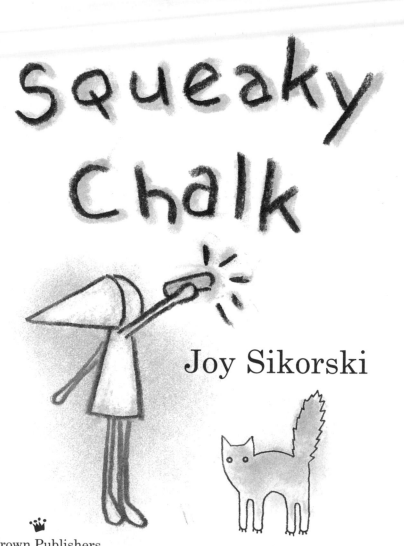

Crown Publishers
New York

Alexander Hamilton's City

*A*lexander Hamilton founded a city in 1792 with the idea that it would become America's first manufacturing center. The success of his city required that its youngest citizens, its children, work in factories with their mothers.

Hamilton's city became famous for the manufacture of cotton, steam-powered locomotive engines, and the legendary Colt revolvers. But it was the manufacture of silk that gave Hamilton's city great wealth and its favorite nickname, which is Silk City. To this day, Silk City's emblem depicts a boy planting a mulberry tree. Mulberry leaves are the silkworm's favorite food.

Left: *Alexander Hamilton* by John Trumbull
Oil on canvas, 30 3/4" x 24 3/4"
The Metropolitan Museum of Art, gift of Henry G. Marquand (81.11).
Photograph © 1987 The Metropolitan Museum of Art

IF YOU KNOW
HOW TO WRITE,
YOU ALREADY KNOW HOW TO DRAW

Lesson 2
SQUEAKY CHALK

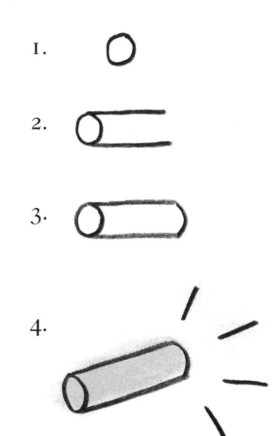

1.

2.

3.

4.

Make your own thinking cap.

Roll up a cone from a large sheet of paper.

Use glue or tape to keep the cone together.

Trim the base with scissors. Tie a string as a guide.

A Thinking Cap

A

1.

2.

3.

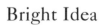

Bright Idea

Lesson 4
A BOY NAMED WIT

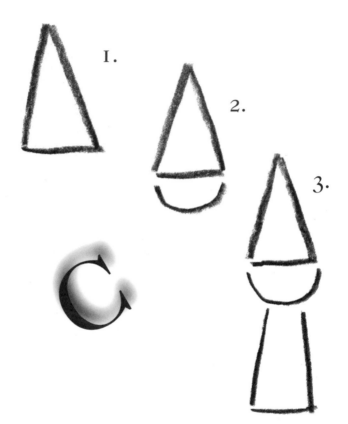

4.

Lesson 5
A CAT NAMED MITT'NS

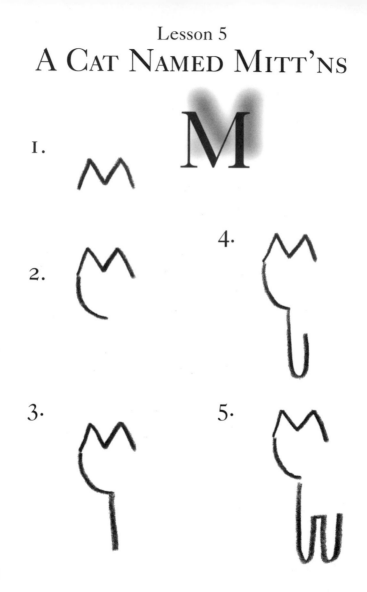

1.

2.

3.

4.

5.

6.

9.

7.

10.

8.

11.

Lesson 6
MULBERRY TREE & BLOSSOM

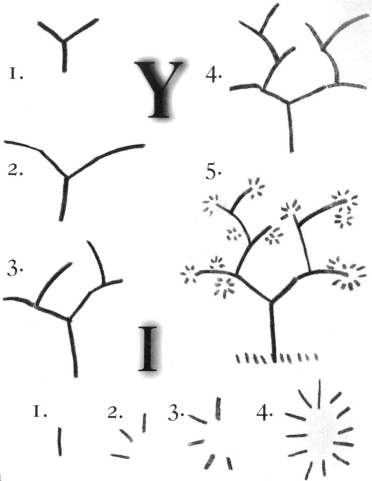

1.

2.

3.

4.

5.

1.

2.

3.

4.

Lesson 7
A Junkyard

SILK CITY SCRAP KEEP OUT

SILK CITY BEE

Silk City to Become "Candy City"

By Mike O'Casey

This morning in the city founded by Alexander Hamilton as a great manufacturing center, the mayor proclaimed that Silk City will become "Candy City." Tartan Sweet Novelty Candy company will open its flagship candy store here. "The future," the mayor said, "is going to be sweet."

Critics of the mayor claim that while the candy store will provide some jobs, tourism would provide many more. People everywhere are more curious about Silk City's history than they are hungry for a piece of candy.

16

Today's Puzzle

Given the following 10 clues, what is happening in the drawing below? The answer is printed at the bottom of this page.

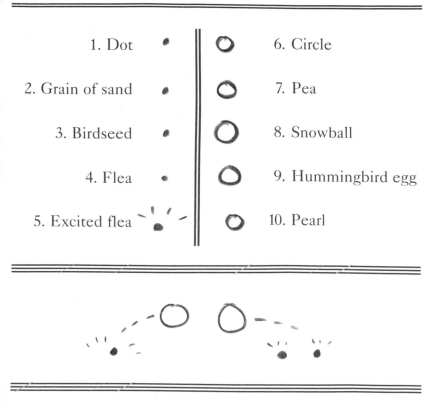

1. Dot
2. Grain of sand
3. Birdseed
4. Flea
5. Excited flea

6. Circle
7. Pea
8. Snowball
9. Hummingbird egg
10. Pearl

Answer: Excited fleas are having a snowball fight.   17

Lesson 8
A TWITTER BIRD

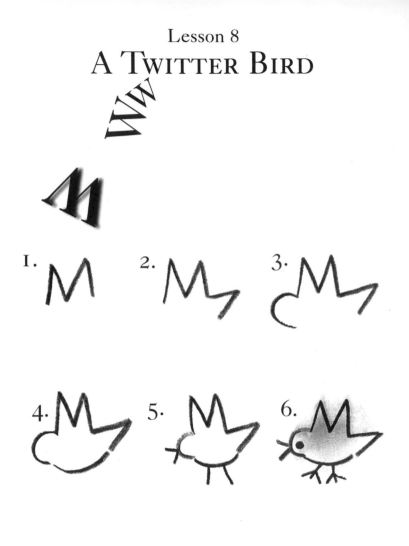

Lesson 9
FLIGHT PATH

I'm so sweet sweet sweet
I'm so sweet sweet sweet
sweet! sweet! sweet! sweet!

Lesson 10
KITE

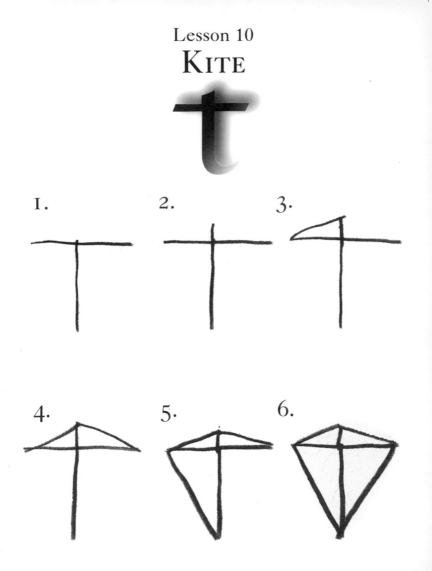

1.

2.

3.

4.

5.

6.

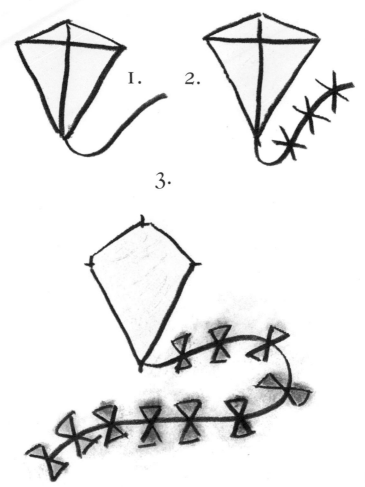

1.

2.

3.

Lesson 12
KITE IN THE AIR

Do you believe it?
Do you hear it?
Do you see it?

Lesson 13
KITE CHASE

Here, here, over here!

Here, here, over here!

Here, here, over here!

SPEAK IN SCOTS

win'	means:	wind
'twad	means:	if it was
blawn	means:	blowing
bonny	means:	lovely

"The win' blew as 'twad blawn its last"

Robert Burns, *Tam O'
Shanter, a Tale*

Lesson 14
TAM-O'-SHANTER

1.

2.

3.

4.

*O*n a bonny day in spring, Professor Thistle, the president of Tartan Sweet Novelty Candy, flies a kite over Silk City. He is testing the winds for his newest invention, a candy called Pegasus.

TARTAN SWEET
NOVELTY CANDY
SILK CITY

TARTAN SWEET
NOVELTY CANDY
SILK CITY

Lesson 15
PLAID

SPARKS

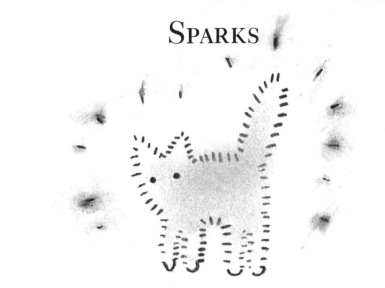

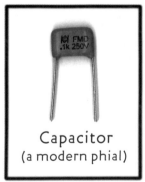

Capacitor
(a modern phial)

*I*n the 1700s, Ben Franklin and other scientists collected electricity, like the kind you get from petting a cat. They stored the electricity in metal-coated glass jars they called "phials."

*B*en Franklin and his contemporaries saw that electrical sparks were similar to lightning. They reasoned that if lightning was also electrical, it could be stored in their phials. A variety of experiments were devised to capture lightning. Ben Franklin's kite experiment is the most famous.

Ben Franklin's Kite

The following is Ben Franklin's letter to Peter Collinson in 1752, describing how he captured lightning using a kite made of silk. It is a dangerous experiment.

s frequent mention is made in public papers from Europe of the success of the Philadelphia experiment for drawing the electrical fire from clouds by means of pointed rods of iron erected on high buildings, &c, it may be agreeable to the curious to be informed that the same experiment has succeeded in Philadelphia, though made in a different and more easy manner, which is as follows:

Make a small cross of two light strips of cedar, the arms so long as to reach to the four corners of a large thin silk handkerchief when extended. Tie the corners of the handkerchief to the extremities of the cross, so you have the body of a kite; which being properly accommodated with a tail, loop, and string, will rise in the air, like those made of paper; but this being of silk is fitter to bear the wet and wind of a thunder gust without tearing.

33

To the top of the upright stick of the cross is to be fixed a very sharp pointed wire, rising a foot or more above the wood. To the end of the

twine, next to the hand, is to be tied a silk ribbon, and where the silk and twine join, a key may be fastened. This kite is to be raised when a thunder gust appears to be coming on, and the person who holds the string must stand within a door, or window, or under some cover, so that the silk ribbon may not be wet; and care must be taken that the twine does not touch the door or window. As soon as any of the thunder clouds come over the kite, the pointed wire will draw the electric fire from them, and the kite, with all the twine, will be electrified, and the loose filaments of the twine will stand out every way, and be attracted by an approaching finger. And when the rain has wet the kite and twine, so that it can conduct electric fire freely, you will find it streams out plentifully from the key on the approach of your knuckle.

Lesson 16
THREE-CORNERED HAT

At this key the phial may be charged; and from electric fire thus obtained, spirits may be kindled, and all the other electric experiments be performed, which are usually done by the help of a rubbed glass globe or tube; and thereby the sameness of the electric matter with that of lightning completely demonstrated.

From *Experiments and Observations on Electricity Made at Philadelphia in America* by Benjamin Franklin, fifth edition, London, 1774, printed for F. Newberry.

Lesson 17
MAKE AN EDDY KITE

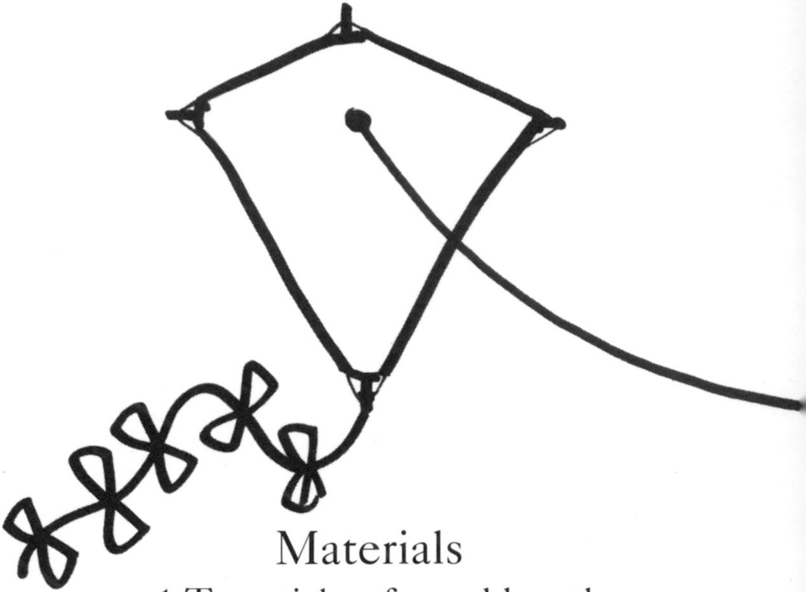

Materials

1. Two sticks of equal length
2. Strong paper of any kind
3. Kite string
4. Glue

Tools

1. Scissors
2. Ruler or tape measure
3. Coping saw or similar fine saw
4. Pencil or a piece of chalk

❶Saw a groove in the ends of each stick. Be careful to keep grooves aligned with each other.

❷Cross the two sticks. The center of the horizontal stick should meet the vertical stick at a point 80 percent from the bottom of the vertical stick. ❸Tie firmly at the axis where they cross. ❹Once the two sticks are crossed, run a piece of string around the perimeter of the sticks, through the grooves. Tie the string to itself. The frame is complete when the crossed sticks are perpendicular to each other and the string is taut.

❺Place the kite frame on a piece of paper having length and width equal to the length and width of your sticks. It should be a square piece of paper.

❻Place a heavy weight on the kite frame while you trace a line two or so inches outside the kite frame string. Cut the paper at this line.

The kite frame lying on the kite paper.

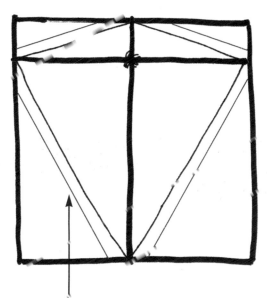

The red line is the line traced on the kite paper. Cut the paper at this line.

❼ Once the paper is cut, fold it over the kite frame string and glue it down.

Right: The kite frame lying on the kite paper after it is cut.

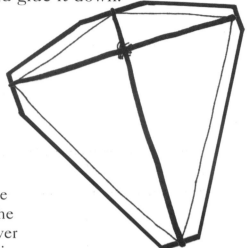

Below: The kite frame lying on the kite paper after the paper is folded over the kite frame string.

The kite with string attached, ready to fly.

Below: The kite
with its horizontal
stick bowed.

FLYING YOUR KITE

❽Stretch a piece of string across the kite's horizontal
stick. Pull tight to make the stick bow. Tie it.
❾Attach your kite string to the kite sticks through
a hole in the paper at the point where the sticks
cross. A tail is optional.
　❿Run with your kite into the wind!

Lesson 18
MULBERRIES!

O

I.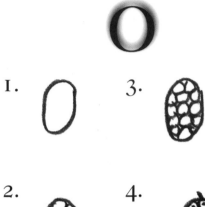

3.

2.

4.

Black or white

Lesson 19
FIREFLY

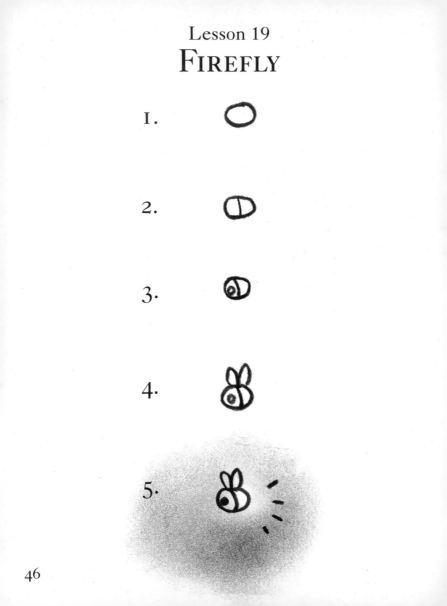

1.

2.

3.

4.

5.

Lesson 20
ASSORTED WORMS

1. 2. 3.

WILD CATS
&
PUSSYCATS

AT THE

SILK CITY
MUSEUM
OF THIS & THAT

48

Lesson 21
FENCE

1.

2.

3.

4.

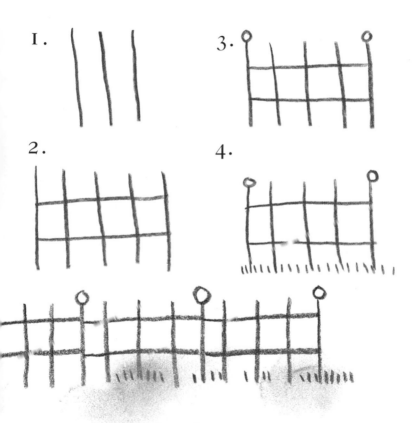

Lesson 22
HUBCAP

1.

2.

3.

4.

WILD CATS
&
PUSSYCATS

AT THE

SILK
CITY
MUSEUM
OF THIS & THAT

Hall of Apes

Hall of Prickles

1.

2.

1.

2.

1.

2.

Lesson 23
PRICKLES

variation:
porcupine
wearing crown

hedgehog

3.   4.

cactus

3.   4.

sea urchin

3.

6.

B C L O

1. B

2.

3. L

4. O L O

5.

6.

7.

8.

9.

10.

Some pterodactyls had 15-foot wingspans. Others were as small as twitter birds.

56

PTERODACTYL

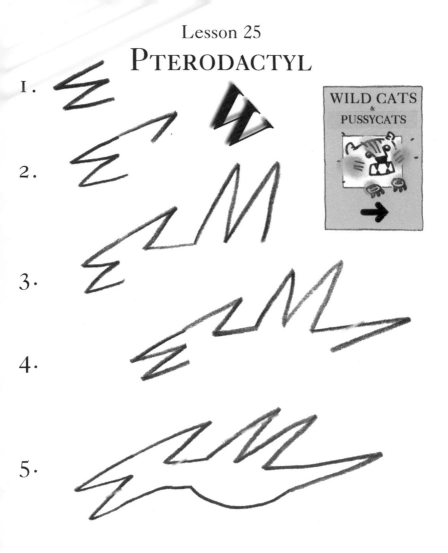

1.

2.

3.

4.

5.

WILD CATS
&
PUSSYCATS

TYRANNOSAURUS REX

1.

2.

3.

4.

5.

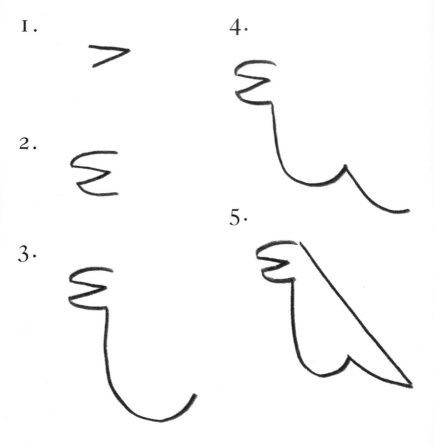

Hall of Dinosaurs

6.

WILD CATS
&
PUSSYCATS

7.

8.

TRICERATOPS

1.

2.

3.

4.

5.

6.

7.

8.

STEGOSAURUS

1.

2.

3.

4.

5.

6.

WILD CATS
&
PUSSYCATS

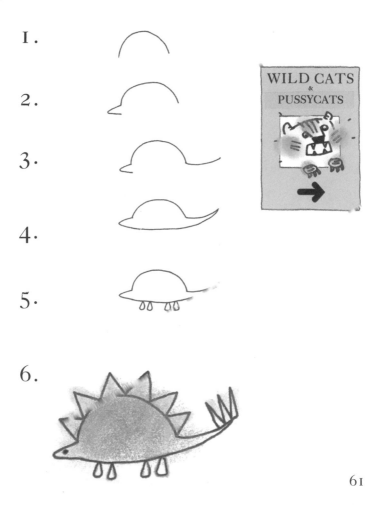

Lesson 29
APATOSAURUS

1.

2.

3.

4.

5.

6.

Professor Huxley tells us a great chapter of the history of the world is written in chalk. "The man who should know the true history of the bit of chalk which every carpenter carries about in his breeches-pocket, though ignorant of all other history, is likely, if he will think his knowledge out to its ultimate results, to have a truer, and therefore a better, conception of this wonderful universe, and of man's relation to it, than the most learned student who is deep-read in the records of humanity and ignorant of those of Nature."

"Chalk, in fact, is a compound of carbonic acid gas, and lime. . . . Powder a little chalk and drop it into a good deal of strong vinegar, there would be a great **bubbling and fizzing,** and, finally, a clear liquid, in which no sign of chalk would appear."—"On a Piece of Chalk," *Macmillan's* magazine, 1868

WILD CATS
&
PUSSYCATS

63

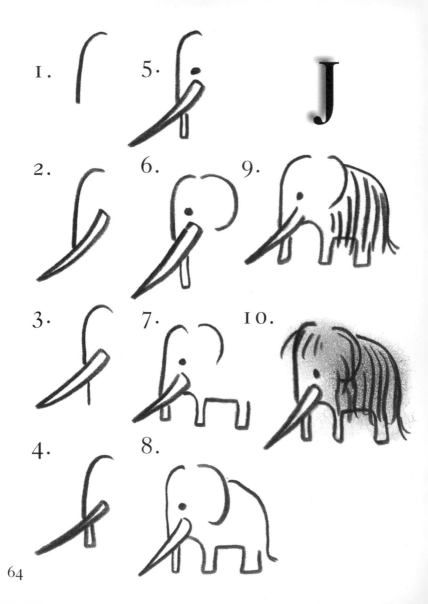

1.

2.

3.

4.

5.

6.

7.

8.

9.

10.

J

Lessons 30 & 31
WOOLLY MAMMOTH

&

A BABY ELEPHANT

G

WILD CATS
&
PUSSYCATS

1.   2.   3.   4.

5.   6.

Sea Monsters

Lesson 32
SHARK

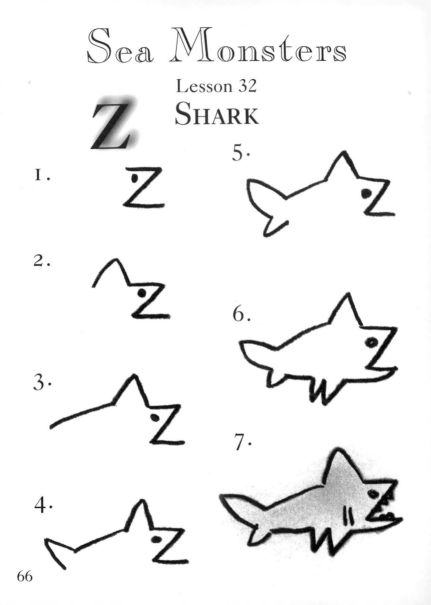

Z

1.

2.

3.

4.

5.

6.

7.

NESSIE

1.

2.

3.

4.

5.

WILD CATS
&
PUSSYCATS

Silk City Museum History Garden

AIRCRAFT
ENGINES

LOCOMOTIVE
ENGINES

SUBMARINES

SILK

69

WILD CATS & PUSSYCATS

It would have made a cat laugh.

Who will bell the cat?

All cats are gray in the dark.

The cat is a symbol of liberty.

70

Lesson 34
TIGER

1.

2.

3.

4.

5.

6.

7.

8.

9.

10.

Y

1.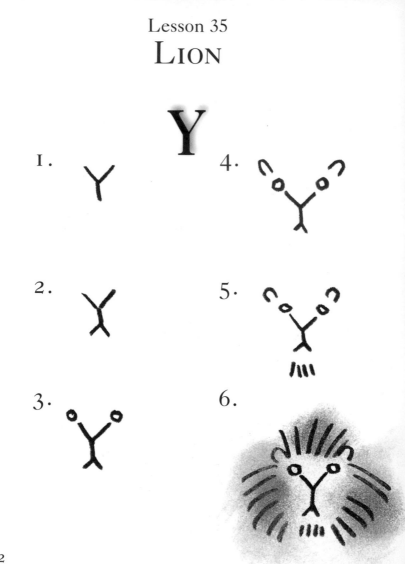

2.

3.

4.

5.

6.

Lesson 36
KITTEN

1.

2.

3.

4.

5.

6.

7.

8.

Rabbit Catchers, soft paste porcelain
Height, 6 7/16" Italian
Naples, (Capodimonte), 1755-1759
The Metropolitan Museum of Art,
The Jack and Belle Linsky Collection, 1982 (1982 60.286)

Lesson 37
CLAY BUNNY

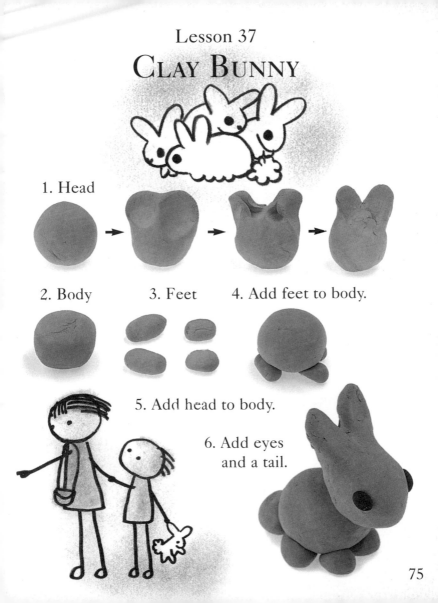

1. Head

2. Body   3. Feet   4. Add feet to body.

5. Add head to body.

6. Add eyes and a tail.

SOUVENIR SHOP

INSTRUCTIONS

1. Cut the Pegasus Ring from the page and snip the red and blue lines to the dots.

2. Twist the ring so that the blue snipped line meets the red snipped line.

3. Slide the snipped lines into each other so that the red and blue dots meet.

PEGASUS BRACELET

AND
PEGASUS RINGS

1.

2.

3.

WILD CAT
&
PUSSYCATS

AT THE

SILK
CITY
MUSEUM
OF THIS & THAT

78

Lesson 38
FENCE SHADOW

Lesson 39
HUBCAP & SHADOW

1.

2.

3.

4.

Could it be that Mitt'ns, a cat born in the junkyard, is descended from the tiger?

Lesson 40
JUNKYARD DOG

1.

2.

3.

4.

5.

6.

7.

8.

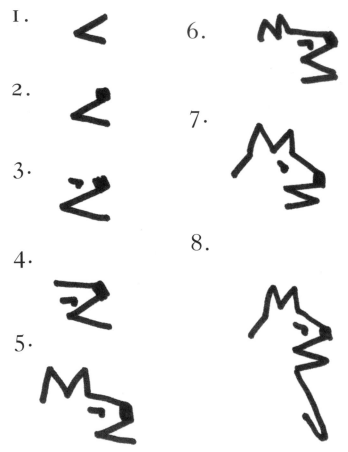

9.

10.

11.

12.

13.

14.

83

PERSEVERING DOG

A boast being made of the obedience of a Newfoundland dog in fetching and carrying, the master put a marked shilling under a large square stone by the road side, and, having ridden on three miles, ordered the dog to go back and fetch it. The dog set off, but did not return the whole day. He had gone to the place, and being unable to turn the stone, sat howling by it. Two horsemen came by and saw his distress, and one of them alighting removed the stone, and finding the shilling, put it in his pocket, not supposing that the dog could possibly be looking for that. The dog followed the horses for upwards of twenty miles, stayed in the room where they supped, got into the bed-room, got the breeches in which the fatal shilling had been put, made his escape with them, and dragged them through mud and mire, hedge and ditch, to his master's house.

SIR ISAAC NEWTON'S DOG

*I*n the back drawing-room in the house of Sir Isaac Newton, St. Martin's Street, Leicester Square, the manuscript of his work, the "New Theory of Light and Colours," was destroyed by fire, caused by a favourite little dog in Sir Isaac's absence. The name of this canine incendiary was Diamond. The manner in which the accident occurred is thus related:—The animal was wantoning about the philosopher's study, when it knocked down a candle, and set fire to a heap of manuscript calculations upon which he had been employed for years. The loss was irretrievable; but Sir Isaac only exclaimed with simplicity, "Ah, Diamond, Diamond, you little know what mischief you have been doing!"

"Persevering Dog" and "Sir Isaac Newton's Dog" are from *Ten Thousand Wonderful Things, Comprising whatever is Marvellous and Rare, Curious, Eccentric and Extraordinary in all Ages and Nations*, edited by Edmund Fillingham King, M.A., George Routledge and Sons Limited, London, 1859

Lesson 41
AUTUMN LEAF

1.

2.

3.

4.

5.

6.

7.

variation:

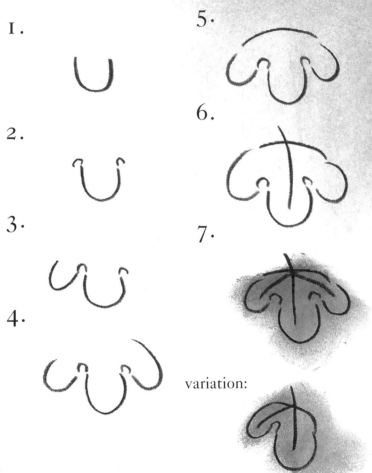

A GIRL NAMED PATIENCE

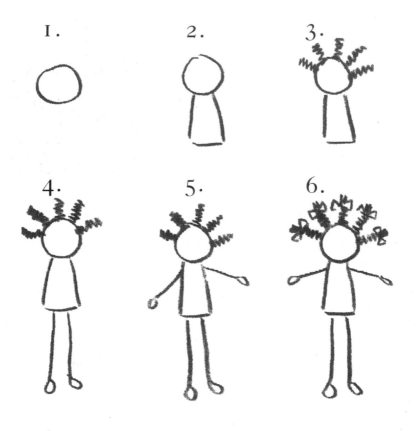

Lesson 43
SNAIL OR FANCY HAT

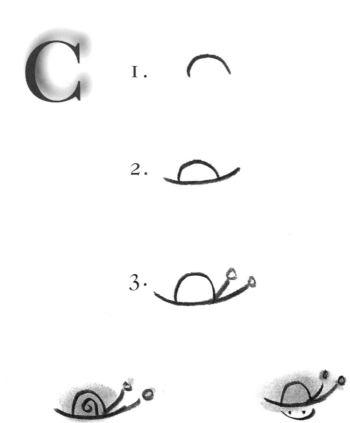

1.

2.

3.

Lesson 44
HAIRSTYLES

Lesson 45
CAKE

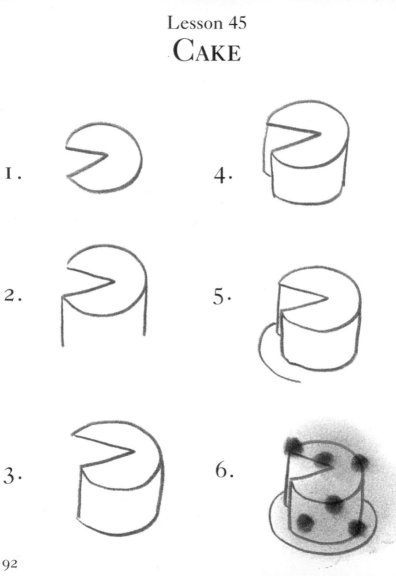

1.

2.

3.

4.

5.

6.

Lesson 46
POLKA-DOT ICING

*B*uy a plain 6" cake from the bakery and make your own polka-dot icing. You will need about three sticks of butter and two boxes of powdered sugar.

Let the butter soften at room temperature. Then stir it until it is very smooth and soft. Stir in powdered sugar a little at a time until very smooth. You can spread the icing with a butter knife.

*F*or the dots, squish raspberries through a strainer so you get the juice and leave the seeds behind. You might have to strain the juice twice. Stir regular white sugar into the raspberry juice until it is like wet sand. Shape it into balls to decorate your cake.

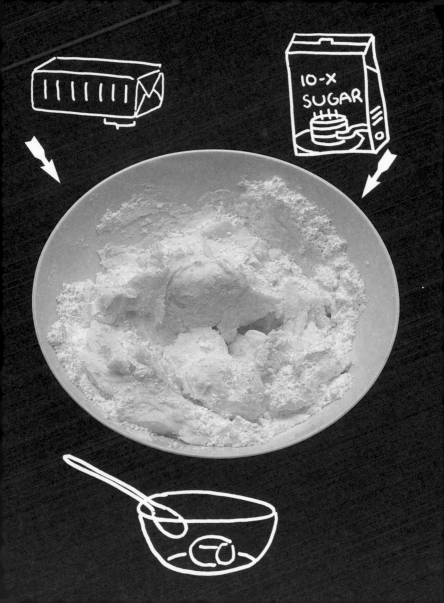

Mulberry Festival

Alexander Hamilton Park, Silk City

Design Contest

Show your plans for the
Alexander Hamilton Memorial

Cake Walk—Win a Polka-Dot Cake

Lesson 47
Map
Historic District
Silk City

Bridge

Lenape River

L'Enfant Falls

Junkyard

Middle Canal

Site of the Alexander Hamilton Memorial

Silk City Museum

Alexander Hamilton Park

Tartan Sweet Novelty Candy

Lesson 48
PARTY BOAT

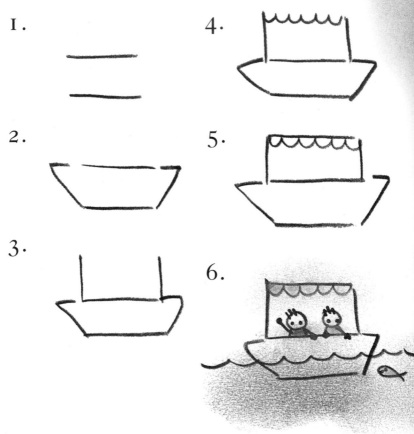

1.

2.

3.

4.

5.

6.

Lesson 49
BEAVER

1.

2.

3.

4.

5.

6.

7.

8.

9.

10.

BEAVER LODGE & STUMP

1.   2.   3.   4.

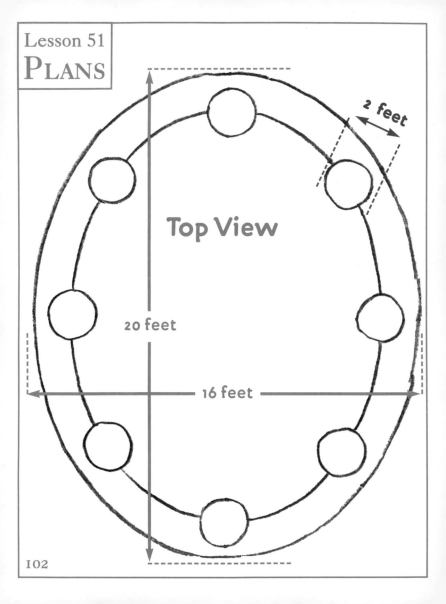

Top View

2 feet

20 feet

16 feet

The Alexander Hamilton Memorial

Alexander Hamilton Park, Silk City

RE WRITTEN, AS WITH A SUNBEAM, IN THE WHOLE

Lesson 52
DIG A HOLE

Silk City Toys Unearthed

Clay doll
heads

Key

Jingle bell

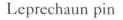

Clay marble

Leprechaun pin

Clay bubble pipe

Photographed by Juliette Gerhardt of John Milner Associates, Inc.
Reproduced with permission of the Federal Highway Administration
and the New Jersey Department of Transportation.

Lesson 53
SPINNING TOP

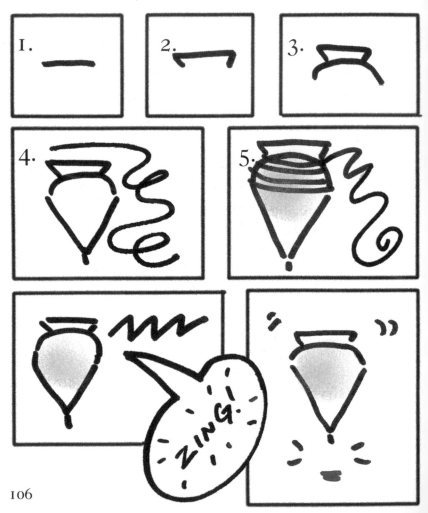

Lesson 54
BUBBLE

1.

2.

3.

Lesson 55
SWING

1.

2.

3.

4.

5.

6.

7.

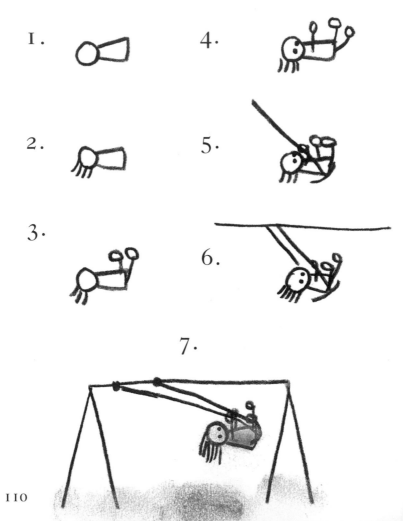

Lesson 56
WHEEL LOADER

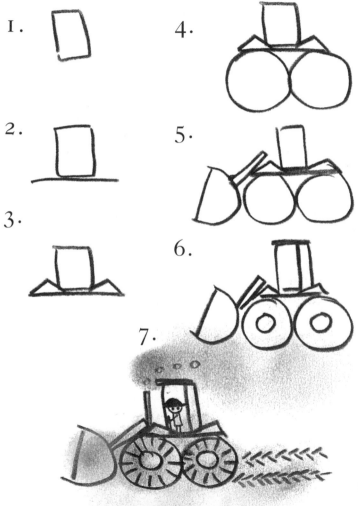

1.

2.

3.

4.

5.

6.

7.

Lesson 57
SMOKE

Madge Madge Madge
put on your tea kettle-ettle-ettle
tea kettle-ettle-ettle
ettle-ettle

1.

2.

3.

4.

5.

6.

7.

SILK CITY BEE

Bubbles Pop in Silk City

By Mike O'Casey

That pesky inventor is at it again. Professor Thistle, Tartan Sweet president and chief candy inventor, said that it was his bubbles that brought a surprise ending to the Silk City Mulberry Festival yesterday, snarling traffic.

"I was just testing the winds. Pegasus Candy will fly in a day or two," the professor said.

Kids Dig Up Old Toys

Kids poking around the Alexander Hamilton Memorial construction site found old toys and other old items. Shown here are glass teddy bear eyes and a brass button from a coachman's jacket. The Silk City Museum accepted the items for a future exhibit.

Today's Thoughtful Comic

Let us suppose that with advances in genetic engineering, a blob of candy can be created that can, in effect, grow by consuming ordinary matter. Could there be a problem with such a new candy product?

Lesson 58
SNOW

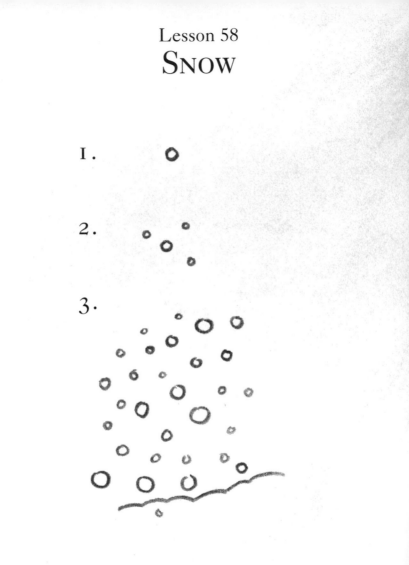

1.

2.

3.

Lesson 59
SNOWFLAKE

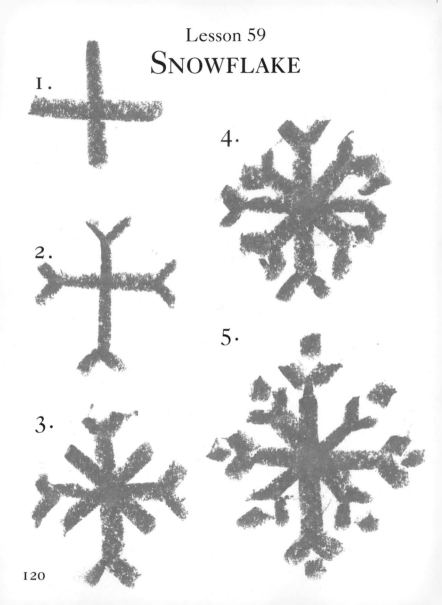

1.

2.

3.

4.

5.

Lesson 60
HORSE

1.

2.

3.

4.

5.

6.

7.

8.

9.

10.

11.

Lesson 61
WINGS

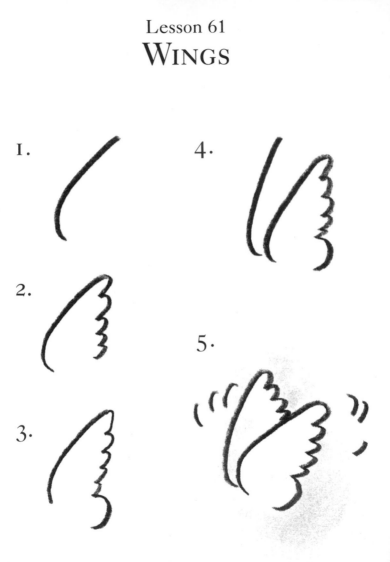

1.

2.

3.

4.

5.

Lesson 62
PEGASUS

The winged horse of Greek and Roman mythology.

Make anything fly by adding wings!

Nessie flying.

Lesson 63
FAIRY

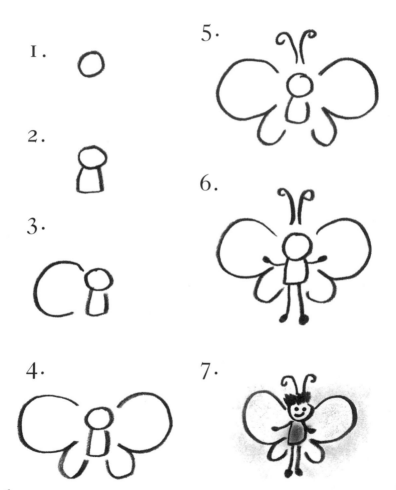

1.

2.

3.

4.

5.

6.

7.

Fairy: a supernatural being, fond of pranks, but generally pleasing.

Fairy money: found money. Said to be placed by some good fairy at the spot where it was picked up. "Fairy money" is apt to change into leaves.

Gnome:

the guardian of mines, quarries, etc.

Nix: (female, nixie) a water spirit. The nix has green teeth and wears a green hat; the nixie is very beautiful.

Oberon: King of the Fairies.

Pigwidgeon: a fairy of very diminutive size.

Puck: a merry little fairy spirit full of fun and harmless mischief.

Wood nymph:

each tree has its own wood nymph, who dies when the tree dies.

PEGASUS CANDY FLIES TODAY!

Where, where, all together down the hill

Where, where, all together down the hill

Where, where, all together down the hill

Lesson 64
PEGASUS CANDY

1.

2.

3.

4.

5.

6.

Lesson 65
SLED

1.

S

2.

3.

4.

5.

6.

7.

8.

9.

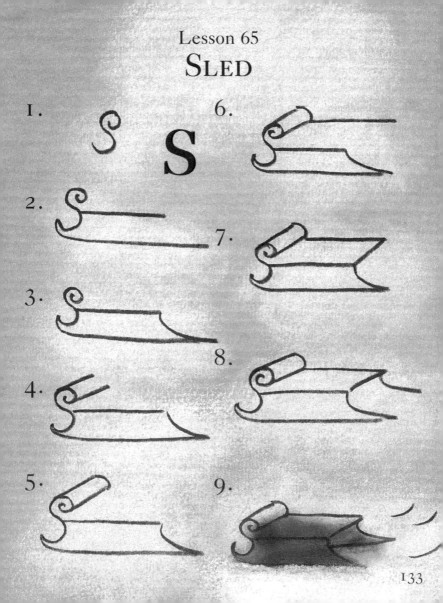

Lesson 66
MOGUL
(SNOW BUMP)

1.

2.

3.

4.

5.

6.

7.

a mogul caused by a
hibernating bear

At the bottom of Weasel Mountain, Pegasus Candies were everywhere, but they were impossible to catch.

$\mathcal{P}$egasus Candies were flying all over Silk City with the same result . . . no one could catch them!

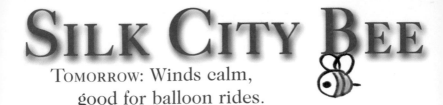

Candy Dream Out of Reach

By Mike O'Casey

Early today, little Pegasus-shaped candy forms were seen flying everywhere in Silk City. The Tartan Sweet Novelty Candy Company released trailer truck loads of the flying sweet steeds. Unfortunately, none could be corralled.

"I caught one," claimed a boy, "but it leapt up and got away." Other kids had similar stories.

Today's high winds may be to blame, but the thought on everyone's mind was the same: no one will want to buy candy that is impossible to catch.

We are reminded of what the Scottish poet Robert Burns said to a mouse in 1785, **"The best laid schemes o' mice and men gang aft agley."** Gang aft a-gley means "go often wrong."

Sightings Around Town

Above: *The Snail*, Vik Muniz, 1993, toned gelatin silver print, 20" by 24".
The Metropolitan Museum of Art

"Haven't you sometimes
seen a cloud that looked
like a centaur? Or a
leopard perhaps? Or a
wolf? Or a bull?"
Aristophanes (423 B.C.), *The
Clouds.* translated by Dudley Fitts

*P*rofessor Thistle abandoned his invention of flying candy. Instead, he offered balloon rides over Silk City's historic district.

Tourists from all over the world began to visit. High up in the balloon, they could easily see the old factories where children and their mothers worked with Alexander Hamilton to establish manufacturing in America.

PARACHUTE

1.   2.   3.

here are those for whom American history or soaring in a balloon means nothing. On this flight, Mitt'ns just wanted to get back to the junkyard. But how to get him there?

Wit had a bright idea!

Squeaky Chalk

C halks come in all shapes and colors. Some are square and some are round. Some are very hard and some are very soft and crumbly. Just remember, the harder the chalk, the easier it is to make it squeak!

A rtists' chalks are called "pastels". They can be found in art supply stores. I used pastels to color the drawings in *Squeaky Chalk*.

H ere I used a blue pastel to color the sky and a beige pastel to color Mitt'ns's basket. An almost black pastel colors Twitter, who is now escorting Mitt'ns down to earth, back to Silk City and their junkyard home.

T witter, Wit, and Mitt'ns will soon discover that the junkyard is built on an ancient Indian village, a story I will tell in my next *Squeaky Chalk*!

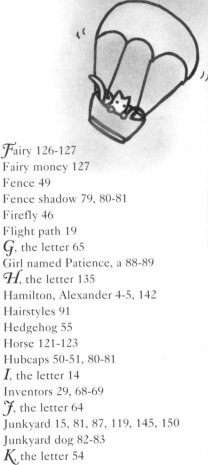

I worked in my father's factory at an early age. I sharpened pencils and played on the typewriter. Meanwhile, out in the back, big pots of metal boiled. Later in life, I picked apples in an orchard. Now I write and draw.

Joy Sikorski

My other books are:

How to Draw a Clam
the Wonderful Vacation Planner

How to Draw a Cup of Coffee
and Other Fun Ideas for Home & Garden

How to Draw a Radish
and Other Fun Things to Do at Work

COLOPHON
The fonts used in
Squeaky Chalk are:

Caslon

*C*aslon *E*xpert
*S*wash *I*talics

Engine

𝔅odoni ℭlassic
𝔅ambus 𝔍nitials

𝔍 dedicate
Squeaky Chalk
with thanks
to my teachers.

SILK CITY
SCRAP